The Steps to **Freedom in Christ**

THE WHOLE GOSPEL

God created Adam and Eve in His image and in His likeness. They were both physically and spiritually alive. Being spiritually alive meant that their souls were in union with God. Living in a dependent relationship with their Heavenly Father, they were to rule over the birds of the sky, the beasts of the field, and the fish of the sea. They were accepted, secure, and significant. However, acting independently of God, they chose to disobey Him and their choice to sin separated them from God. They immediately felt fearful, anxious, depressed, and insecure. Because Eve was deceived by Satan and because Adam sinned, all their descendants are born physically alive, but spiritually dead (Ephesians 2:1). Since all have sinned (Romans 3:23), those who remain separated from God will struggle with personal and spiritual conflicts. Satan became the rebel holder of authority, and the god of this world. Jesus referred to him as the ruler of this world, and the Apostle John wrote that the whole world lies in the power of the evil one (1 John 5:19).

Jesus came to undo the works of Satan (1 John 3:8), and take upon Himself the sins of the world. By dying for our sins, Jesus removed the barrier that existed between God and those He created in His image. The resurrection of Christ brought new life to those who put their trust in Him. Every born-again believer's soul is again in union with God and that is most often communicated in the New Testament with the prepositional phrases "in Christ," or "in Him." The Apostle Paul explained that anyone who is in Christ is a new creation (2 Corinthians 5:17). The Apostle John wrote, "But as many as received Him, to them He gave the right to become children of God, to those who believe in His name" (John 1:12, NKJV), and he also wrote, "See how great a love the Father has bestowed on us, that we would be called children of God; and such we are" (1 John 3:1).

No amount of effort on your part can save you, and neither can any religious activity, no matter how well intentioned. We are saved by faith, that is, by what we choose to believe. All that remains for us to do is put our trust in the finished work of Christ. "For by grace you have been saved through faith; and that not of yourself, it is the gift of God; not as a result of works, so that no one may boast" (Ephesians 2:8–9). If you have never received Jesus as your Lord and Saviour, you can do so right now. God knows the thoughts and intentions of your heart, so all you have to do is put your trust in God alone. You can express your decision in prayer as follows:

Dear Heavenly Father, thank You for sending Jesus to die on the cross for my sins. I acknowledge that I have sinned and that I cannot save myself. I believe that Jesus came to give me life and by faith I now choose to receive You into my life as my Lord and Saviour. May the power of Your indwelling presence enable me to be the person You created me to be. I pray that You would grant me repentance leading to a knowledge of the truth so that I can experience my freedom in Christ and be transformed by the renewing of my mind. In Jesus' precious name I pray. Amen.

ASSURANCE OF SALVATION

Paul wrote, "If you confess with your mouth Jesus as Lord, and believe in your heart that God raised Him from the dead, you will be saved" (Romans 10:9). Do you believe that God the Father raised Jesus from the dead? Did you invite Jesus to be your Lord and Saviour? Then you are a child of God and nothing can separate you from the love of Christ (Romans 8:35). "And the testimony is this, that God has given us eternal life, and this life is in His Son. He who has the Son has the life; he who does not have the Son of God does not have the life" (1 John 5:11–12). Your Heavenly Father has sent His Holy Spirit to bear witness with your spirit that you are a child of God (Romans 8:16). "You were sealed *in Him* with the Holy Spirit of promise" (Ephesians 1:13). The Holy Spirit will guide you into all truth (John 16:13).

12.621

Since we are all born dead (spiritually) in our trespasses and sin (Ephesians 2:1), we had neither the presence of God in our lives nor the knowledge of His ways. Consequently, we all learned to live independently of God. When we became new creations in Christ our minds were not instantly renewed. That is why Paul wrote, "Do not conform any longer to the pattern of this world, but be transformed by the renewing of your mind. Then you will be able to test and approve what God's will is — His good, pleasing, and perfect will" (Romans 12:2 NIV). That is why new Christians struggle with many of the same old thoughts and habits. Their minds have been previously programmed to live independently of God and that is the chief characteristic of our flesh. As new creations in Christ we have the mind of Christ, and the Holy Spirit will lead us into all truth.

To experience our freedom in Christ, and grow in the grace of God, requires repentance, which literally means a change of mind. God will enable that process as we submit to Him and resist the devil (James 4:7). *The Steps to Freedom in Christ* (the *Steps*) are designed to help you do that. Submitting to God is the critical issue. He is the wonderful counsellor and the One who grants repentance leading to a knowledge of the truth (2 Timothy 2:25). The *Steps* cover seven critical issues that affect our relationship with God. We will not experience our freedom in Christ if we seek false guidance, believe lies, fail to forgive others as we have been forgiven, live in rebellion, respond in pride, fail to acknowledge our sin, and continue in the sins of our ancestors. "He who conceals transgressions will not prosper, but he who confesses and forsakes [renounces] them will find compassion" (Proverbs 28:13). "Therefore since we have this ministry, as we received mercy, we do not lose heart, but we renounced things hidden because of shame, not walking in craftiness or adulterating the word of God, but by the manifestation of truth" (2 Corinthians 4:1–2).

Even though Satan is defeated, he still rules this world through a hierarchy of demons who tempt, accuse, and deceive those who fail to put on the armour of God, stand firm in their faith, and take every thought captive to the obedience of Christ. Our sanctuary is our identity and position in Christ and we have all the protection we need to live a victorious life, but if we fail to assume our responsibility and give ground to Satan, we will suffer the consequences of our sinful attitudes and actions. The good news is, we can repent and reclaim all that we have in Christ, and that is what the *Steps* will enable you to do.

PROCESSING THE STEPS

Ideally, it would be best if you attended *The Freedom In Christ Course,* or read *Victory Over The Darkness,* and *The Bondage Breaker* before you process the *Steps.* Books, audio, and video resources are available from Freedom In Christ Ministries (www.ficminternational.org). The best way to go through the *Steps* is to process them with a trained encourager. The book, *Discipleship Counseling,* explains the theology and process. You can also go through the *Steps* on your own. Every step is explained so you will have no trouble doing that. I suggest you find a quiet place where you can process the *Steps* out loud. If you experience some mental interference, just ignore it and continue on. Thoughts such as, *This isn't going to work,* or *I don't believe this,* or blasphemous, condemning, and accusing thoughts have no power over you unless you believe them. They are just thoughts and it doesn't make any difference if they originate from yourself, an external source, or from Satan and his demons. They will be resolved when you have fully repented. If you are working through the *Steps* with an encourager, share any mental or physical opposition that you are experiencing. The mind is the control centre, and you will not lose control in the freedom appointment if you don't lose control of your mind. The best way to do that, if you are being mentally harassed, is to just share it. Exposing the lies to the light breaks the power.

The Apostle Paul wrote that "Satan disguises himself as an angel of light" (2 Corinthians 11:14). It is not uncommon for some to have thoughts or hear voices that claim to be friendly, offer companionship, or claim to be from God. They may even say that Jesus is Lord, but they cannot say that Jesus is *their* Lord. If there is any doubt about their origin, verbally ask God to show you the true nature of such spirit guides. You don't want any spirit guide other than the Holy Spirit to guide you.

Remember, you are a child of God and seated with Christ in the heavenlies (spiritual realm). That means you have the authority and power to do His will. The *Steps* don't set you free. Jesus sets you free and you will progressively experience that freedom as you respond to Him in faith and repentance. Don't worry about any demonic interference, most do not experience any. It doesn't make any difference if Satan has a little role or a bigger role, the critical issue is your relationship with God and that is what you are resolving. This is a ministry of reconciliation. Once those issues are resolved, Satan has no right to remain. Successfully completing this repentance process is not an end, it is a beginning of growth. Unless these issues are resolved, however, the growth process will be stalled and your Christian life will be stagnant.

BREAKING MENTAL STRONGHOLDS

On a separate piece of paper write down any false beliefs and lies that surface during the *Steps*, especially those that are not true about yourself and God. When you are finished, verbally say for each exposed falsehood: *I renounce the lie that (what you have believed)*, and *I announce the truth that (what you are now choosing to believe is true based on God's word)*. It may be best to have the encourager keep this list for you if you are being led by another through the *Steps*. It is strongly recommended that you repeat the process of renouncing lies and choosing truth for forty days since we are transformed by the renewing of our minds (Romans 12:2), and it is very easy to defer back to old flesh patterns when tempted.

PREPARATION

Processing these *Steps* will play a major role in your journey of becoming more and more like Jesus so that you can be a fruitful disciple. The purpose is to become firmly rooted in Christ. It doesn't take long to establish your identity and freedom in Christ, but there is no such thing as instant maturity. Renewing your mind and conforming to the image of God is a lifelong process. May God grace you with His presence as you seek to do His will. Once you have experienced your freedom in Christ you can help others experience the joy of their salvation.

You are now ready to begin the *Steps* by saying the prayer and declaration on the following page.

PRAYER

Dear Heavenly Father, You are present in this room and in my life. You alone are all-knowing, all-powerful and everywhere present and I worship You alone. I declare my dependency upon You, for apart from You I can do nothing. I choose to believe Your Word, which teaches that all authority in heaven and on earth belongs to the resurrected Christ, and being alive in Christ I have the authority to resist the devil as I submit to You. I ask that You fill me with Your Holy Spirit and guide me into all truth. I ask for Your complete protection and guidance as I seek to know You and do Your will. In the wonderful name of Jesus I pray. Amen.

DECLARATION

In the name and authority of the Lord Jesus Christ, I command Satan and all evil spirits to release their hold on me in order that I can be free to know and choose to do the will of God. As a child of God who is seated with Christ in the heavenly places, I declare that every enemy of the Lord Jesus Christ in my presence be bound. God has not given me a spirit of fear, therefore I reject any and all condemning, accusing, blasphemous, and deceiving spirits of fear. Satan and all his demons cannot inflict any pain or in any way prevent God's will from being done in my life today, because I belong to the Lord Jesus Christ.

REVIEW OF YOUR LIFE

Before going through the *Steps*, review the following events of your life to discern specific areas that need to be addressed:

Family History

- ❏ Religious history of parents and grandparents
- ❏ Home life from childhood through high school
- ❏ History of physical or emotional illness in the family
- ❏ Adoption, foster care, guardians

Personal History

- ❏ Eating habits (bulimia, anorexia, compulsive eating)
- ❏ Addictions (smoking, drugs, alcohol, gambling)
- ❏ Prescription medications (what for?)
- ❏ Sleeping patterns, dreams, and nightmares
- ❏ Rape or any other sexual, physical, mental, or emotional abuse
- ❏ Thought life (obsessive, blasphemous, condemning, and distracting thoughts; poor concentration; fantasy; suicidal; fearful; jealous; confused; guilt and shame)
- ❏ Mental interference during church, prayer, or Bible study
- ❏ Emotional life (anger, anxiety, depression, bitterness, and fear)
- ❏ Spiritual journey (salvation: when, how, and assurance)
- ❏ Any other traumatic experience

STEP 1
COUNTERFEIT VERSUS REAL

The first step towards experiencing your freedom in Christ is to renounce (verbally reject) all involvement (past or present) with occult, cult, or false religious teachings or practices. Participation in any group that denies that Jesus Christ is Lord and/or elevates any teaching or book to the level of (or above) the Bible must be renounced. In addition, groups that require dark, secret initiations, ceremonies, vows, pacts, or covenants need to be renounced. God does not take lightly false guidance. "As for the person who turns to mediums and to spiritists... I will also set My face against that person and will cut him off from among My people" (Leviticus 20:6). Ask God to guide you as follows:

> Dear Heavenly Father, please bring to my mind anything and everything that I have done knowingly or unknowingly that involves occult, cult or false religious teachings and practices. Grant me the wisdom and grace to renounce any and all spiritual counterfeits, false religious teachings, and practices. In Jesus' name I pray. Amen.

The Lord may bring events to your mind that you have forgotten, even experiences you participated in as a game or thought were a joke. You might even have been passively or curiously watching others participate in counterfeit religious practices. The purpose is to renounce all counterfeit spiritual experiences and associated beliefs that God brings to your mind. Use the following "Non-Christian Spiritual Experience Checklist" as a guide. Then pray the prayer following the checklist to renounce each activity or group the Lord brings to mind. He may reveal to you counterfeit spiritual experiences that are not on the list. Be especially aware of your need to renounce non-Christian religious practices that were part of your culture growing up. It is important that you prayerfully renounce them.

NON-CHRISTIAN SPIRITUAL EXPERIENCE CHECKLIST

Select all those that you have participated in:

- ❏ Out-of-body experiences
- ❏ Wicca
- ❏ Ouija board
- ❏ Black and white magic/The Gathering
- ❏ Bloody Mary
- ❏ Paganism
- ❏ Charlie Charlie
- ❏ Reiki
- ❏ Occult games such as light as a feather
- ❏ Channeling/Chakras
- ❏ Magic eight ball
- ❏ Reincarnation/previous life healing
- ❏ Table or body lifting
- ❏ Mediums and channelers
- ❏ Spells and curses
- ❏ Mormonism

- ❏ Mental telepathy/mind control
- ❏ Freemasonry
- ❏ Tarot cards
- ❏ Jehovah's Witness (Watchtower)
- ❏ Levitation
- ❏ Christian Science
- ❏ Automatic writing
- ❏ Church of Scientology
- ❏ Astrology/horoscopes
- ❏ Nature worship (Mother earth)
- ❏ Palm reading
- ❏ Unitarianism/universalism
- ❏ Fortune telling/divination
- ❏ Hinduism/Transcendental Meditation
- ❏ Blood pacts

- ❏ Silva Mind Control
- ❏ Sexual spirits
- ❏ Buddhism (including Zen)
- ❏ Séances and circles
- ❏ Islam
- ❏ Trances
- ❏ Witchcraft/sorcery
- ❏ Spirit guides
- ❏ Bahaism
- ❏ Clairvoyance
- ❏ Spiritism/animism/folk religions
- ❏ Rod and pendulum (dowsing)
- ❏ Ancestor worship
- ❏ Hypnosis
- ❏ Satanism (see appendix A)
- ❏ Others: _____

Once you have completed your checklist, confess and renounce every false religious practice, belief, ceremony, vow, or pact that you were involved in by praying the following prayer **aloud**. Take your time and be thorough. Give God time to remind you of every specific incident or ritual as needed:

> **Dear Heavenly Father, I confess that I have participated in** (specifically name every belief and involvement with all that you have selected above) **and I renounce them all as counterfeits. I pray that You will fill me with Your Holy Spirit that I may be guided by You. Thank You that in Christ I am forgiven. Amen.**

Additional Questions to Help You Become Aware of Counterfeit Religious Experiences:

Now consider the following questions and use the words in bold to renounce any issue that God brings to your mind.

1. Do you now have, or have you ever had, an imaginary friend, spirit guide, or "angel" offering you guidance or companionship? If it has a name, renounce it by name. **I renounce...**

2. Have you ever seen or been contacted by beings you thought were aliens from another world? Such deceptions should be identified and renounced. **I renounce...**

3. Have you ever heard voices in your head or had repeating, nagging thoughts (such as *I'm dumb, I'm ugly, Nobody loves me,* or *I can't do anything right*)—as if there were a conversation going on inside your head? **I renounce all deceiving spirits and the lies I have believed** (specify the lies)**...**

4. Have you ever been hypnotized, attended a New Age seminar, consulted a psychic, medium/channeller, or spiritist? Renounce all specific false prophecies and guidance they offered. **I renounce...**

5. Have you ever made a secret covenant, or vow to any organization, or persons other than God, or made an inner vow contrary to scripture (for example, "I will never . . ."). Renounce it. **I renounce...**

6. Have you ever been involved in a satanic ritual or attended a concert in which Satan was the focus? See appendix A for more complete resolution. **I renounce...**

7. Have you ever made any sacrifices to idols, false gods, or spirits? Renounce each one. **I renounce...**

8. Have you ever attended any counterfeit religious event or entered a non-Christian shrine that required you to participate in their religious observances such as washing your hands, or removing your shoes? Confess your participation and renounce your participation in false worship. **I confess... and I renounce...**

9. Have you ever consulted a shaman or witch doctor for the purpose of manipulating the spiritual world to place curses, seek psychic healing, or guidance? All such activity needs to be renounced. **I renounce...**

10. Have you ever tried to contact the dead in order to send or receive messages? Renounce such practices. **I renounce...**

STEP 2
DECEPTION VERSUS TRUTH

The Christian life is lived by faith according to what God says is true. Jesus is the truth, the Holy Spirit is the Spirit of truth, God's word is truth, and we are to speak the truth in love (see John 14:6; 16:13; 17:17; Ephesians 4:15). The biblical response to truth is faith regardless of whether we feel it is true or not. Christians are to forsake all lying, deceiving, or stretching of the truth, and anything else associated with falsehood. Believing lies will keep us in bondage. Choosing to believe the truth is what sets us free (John 8:32). David wrote, "How blessed [happy] is the man . . . in whose spirit there is no deceit" (Psalm 32:2). The liberated Christian is free to walk in the light, and speak the truth in love.

We can be honest and transparent before God, because we are already forgiven, and God already knows the thoughts and intentions of our hearts (Hebrews 4:13). So why not be honest and confess our sins? Confession means to agree with God. People in bondage are tired of living a lie. Because of God's great love and forgiveness we can walk in the light and fellowship with God and others (see 1 John 1:7–9). Begin this commitment to truth by praying the following prayer out loud. Don't let any opposing thoughts, such as *This is a waste of time* or *I wish I could believe this, but I can't*, keep you from pressing forward. God will strengthen you as you rely on Him.

> **Dear Heavenly Father, You are the truth and I desire to live by faith according to Your truth. The truth will set me free, but in many ways I have been deceived by the father of lies, the philosophies of this fallen world, and I have deceived myself. I choose to walk in the light, knowing that You love and accept me just as I am. As I consider areas of possible deception, I invite the Spirit of truth to guide me into all truth. Please protect me from all deception as You "search me, O God, and know my heart; try me and know my anxious thoughts; and see if there be any hurtful way in me, and lead me in the everlasting way" (Psalm 139:23–24). In the name of Jesus I pray. Amen.**

Prayerfully consider the lists in the three exercises over the page, using the prayers at the end of each exercise in order to confess any ways you have given in to deception or wrongly defended yourself. You cannot instantly renew your mind, but the process will never get started without acknowledging your mental strongholds or defence mechanisms, also known as flesh patterns.

WAYS YOU CAN BE DECEIVED BY THE WORLD

- ❑ Believing that having an abundance of money and possessions will make me happy (Matthew 13:22; 1 Timothy 6:10)
- ❑ Believing that eating food, drinking alcohol, or using drugs can relieve my stress and make me happy (Proverbs 23:19 21)
- ❑ Believing that an attractive body, phony personality, or image will meet my needs for acceptance and significance (Proverbs 31:10; 1 Peter 3:3–4)
- ❑ Believing that gratifying sexual lust will bring lasting satisfaction without any negative consequences (Ephesians 4:22; 1 Peter 2:11)
- ❑ Believing that I can sin and suffer no negative consequences (Hebrews 3:12–13)
- ❑ Believing that I need more than Jesus to meet my needs of acceptance, security, and significance (2 Corinthians 11:2–4,13–15)
- ❑ Believing that I can do whatever I want regardless of others and still be free (Proverbs 16:18; Obadiah 3; 1 Peter 5:5)
- ❑ Believing that people who refuse to receive Jesus will go to heaven anyway (1 Corinthians 6:9–11)
- ❑ Believing that I can associate with bad company and not become corrupted (1 Corinthians 15:33–34)
- ❑ Believing that I can read, see, or listen to anything and not be corrupted (Proverbs 4:23–27; Matthew 5:28)
- ❑ Believing that there are no earthly consequences for my sin (Galatians 6:7–8)
- ❑ Believing that I must gain the approval of certain people in order to be happy (Galatians 1:10)
- ❑ Believing that I must measure up to certain religious standards in order for God to accept me (Galatians 3:2–3; 5:1)
- ❑ Believing that there are many paths to God and Jesus is only one of the many ways (John 14:6)
- ❑ Believing that I must live up to worldly standards in order to feel good about myself (1 Peter 2:1–12)

Dear Heavenly Father, I confess that I have been deceived by (confess the items you selected above). **I thank You for Your forgiveness, and I choose to believe Your Word and believe in Jesus who is the Truth. In Jesus' name I pray. Amen.**

WAYS TO DECEIVE YOURSELF

- ❑ Hearing God's Word but not doing what it says (James 1:22)
- ❑ Saying I have no sin (1 John 1:8)
- ❑ Thinking I am something or someone I'm really not (Galatians 6:3)
- ❑ Thinking I am wise in this worldly age (1 Corinthians 3:18–19)
- ❑ Thinking I can be truly religious and not control what I say (James 1:26)
- ❑ Thinking that God is the source of my problems (Lamentations 3:1–24)
- ❑ Thinking I can live successfully without the help of anyone else (1 Corinthians 12:14–20)

Dear Heavenly Father, I confess that I have deceived myself by (confess the items selected above). **Thank You for Your forgiveness. I commit myself to believe only Your truth. In Jesus' name I pray. Amen.**

WAYS TO WRONGLY DEFEND YOURSELF

- ❑ Denial of reality (conscious or unconscious)
- ❑ Fantasy (escaping reality by daydreaming, TV, movies, music, computer or video games, drugs, or alcohol)
- ❑ Emotional insulation (withdrawing from people or keeping people at a distance to avoid rejection)
- ❑ Regression (reverting back to less threatening times)
- ❑ Displaced anger (taking out frustrations on innocent people)
- ❑ Projection (attributing to another what you find unacceptable in yourself)
- ❑ Rationalization (making excuses for my own poor behaviour)
- ❑ Lying (protecting self through falsehoods)
- ❑ Hypocrisy (presenting a false image)

Dear Heavenly Father, I confess that I have wrongly defended myself by (confess the items selected above). **Thank You for Your forgiveness. I trust You to defend and protect me. In Jesus' name I pray. Amen.**

The wrong ways we have employed to shield ourselves from pain and rejection are often deeply ingrained in our lives. You may need additional discipling/counselling to learn how to allow Jesus to be your rock, fortress, deliverer, and refuge (see Psalm 18:1–2). The more you learn how loving, powerful, and protective God is, the more you'll be likely to trust Him. The more you realize how much God unconditionally loves and accepts you, the more you'll be released to be open, honest, and vulnerable (in a healthy way) before God and others.

The New Age movement has twisted the concept of faith by teaching that we make something true by believing it. That is false. We cannot create reality with our minds; only God can do that. Our responsibility is to face reality and choose to believe what God says is true. True biblical faith, therefore, is choosing to believe and act upon what is true, because God has said it is true, and He is the Truth. Faith is something you decide to do, not something you feel like doing. Believing something doesn't make it true; it's already true, therefore we choose to believe it! Truth is not conditioned by whether we choose to believe it or not.

Everybody lives by faith. The only difference between Christian faith and non-Christian faith is the object of our faith. If the object of our faith is not trustworthy or real, then no amount of believing will change that. That's why our faith must be grounded on the solid rock of God's perfect, unchanging character and the truth of His Word.

For two thousand years Christians have known the importance of verbally and publicly declaring truth. Read aloud the following Statements of Truth, and carefully consider what you are professing. You may find it helpful to read them aloud every day for at least six weeks, which will help renew your mind to the truth.

1. I recognize that there is only one true and living God who exists as the Father, Son, and Holy Spirit. He is worthy of all honour, praise, and glory as the One who made all things and holds all things together. (See Exodus 20:2–3; Colossians 1:16–17.)

2. I recognize that Jesus Christ is the Messiah, the Word who became flesh and dwelt among us. I believe that He came to destroy the works of the devil, and that He disarmed the rulers and authorities and made a public display of them, having triumphed over them. (See John 1:1,14; Colossians 2:15; 1 John 3:8.)

3. I believe that God demonstrated His own love for me in that while I was still a sinner, Christ died for me. I believe that He has delivered me from the domain of darkness and transferred me to His kingdom, and in Him I have redemption, the forgiveness of sins. (See Romans 5:8; Colossians 1:13–14.)

4. I believe that I am now a child of God and that I am seated with Christ in the heavenly realms. I believe that I was saved by the grace of God through faith, and that it was a gift and not a result of any works on my part. (See Ephesians 2:6,8,9; 1 John 3:1–3.)

5. I choose to be strong in the Lord and in the strength of His might. I put no confidence in the flesh, for the weapons of warfare are not of the flesh but are divinely powerful for the destruction of strongholds. I put on the full armour of God. I resolve to stand firm in my faith and resist the evil one. (See 2 Corinthians 10:4; Ephesians 6:10–20; Philippians 3:3.)

6. I believe that apart from Christ I can do nothing, so I declare my complete dependence on Him. I choose to abide in Christ in order to bear much fruit and glorify my Father. I announce to Satan that Jesus is my Lord. I reject any and all counterfeit gifts or works of Satan in my life. (See John 15:5,8; 1 Corinthians 12:3.)

7. I believe that the truth will set me free and that Jesus is the truth. If He sets me free, I will be free indeed. I recognize that walking in the light is the only path of true fellowship with God and man. Therefore, I stand against all of Satan's deception by taking every thought captive in obedience to Christ. I declare that the Bible is the only authoritative standard for truth and life. (See John 8:32,36; 14:6; 2 Corinthians 10:5; 2 Timothy 3:15–17; 1 John 1:3–7.)

8. I choose to present my body to God as a living and holy sacrifice and the members of my body as instruments of righteousness. I choose to renew my mind by the living word of God in order that I may prove that the will of God is good, acceptable, and perfect. I put off the old self with its evil practices and put on the new self. I declare myself to be a new creation in Christ. (See Romans 6:13; 12:1–2; 2 Corinthians 5:17; Colossians 3:9–10.)

9. By faith, I choose to be filled with the Spirit so that I can be guided into all truth. I choose to walk by the Spirit so that I will not carry out the desires of the flesh. (See John 16:13; Galatians 5:16; Ephesians 5:18.)

10. I renounce all selfish goals and choose the ultimate goal of love. I choose to obey the two greatest commandments: to love the Lord my God with all my heart, soul, mind, and strength, and to love my neighbour as myself. (See Matthew 22:37–39; 1 Timothy 1:5.)

11. I believe that the Lord Jesus has all authority in heaven and on earth, and He is the head over all rule and authority. I am complete in Him. I believe that Satan and his demons are subject to me in Christ since I am a member of Christ's body. Therefore, I obey the command to submit to God and resist the devil, and I command Satan in the name of Jesus Christ to leave my presence. (See Matthew 28:18; Ephesians 1:19–23; Colossians 2:10; James 4:7.)

STEP THREE
BITTERNESS VERSUS FORGIVENESS

We are called to be merciful just as our Heavenly Father is merciful (Luke 6:36) and forgive others as we have been forgiven (Ephesians 4:31). Doing so sets us free from our past and doesn't allow Satan to take advantage of us (2 Corinthians 2:10–11). Ask God to bring to your mind the people you need to forgive by praying the following prayer aloud:

> **Dear Heavenly Father, I thank You for the riches of Your kindness, forbearance, and patience towards me, knowing that Your kindness has led me to repentance. I confess that I have not shown that same kindness and patience towards those who have hurt or offended me (Romans 2:4). Instead, I have held on to my anger, bitterness, and resentment towards them. Please bring to my mind all the people I need to forgive in order that I may now do so. In Jesus' name I pray. Amen.**

On a separate sheet of paper, list the names of people who come to your mind. At this point don't question whether you need to forgive them or not. Often we hold things against ourselves as well, punishing ourselves for wrong choices we've made in the past. Write "myself" at the bottom of your list if you need to forgive yourself. Forgiving yourself is accepting the truth that God has already forgiven you in Christ. If God forgives you, you can forgive yourself!

Also write down "thoughts against God" at the bottom of your list. Obviously, God has never done anything wrong so He doesn't need our forgiveness, but we need to let go of our disappointments with our heavenly Father. People often harbour angry thoughts against Him because He did not do what they wanted Him to do. Those feelings of anger or resentment towards God need to be released.

Before you begin working through the process of forgiving those on your list, review what forgiveness is and what it is not. The critical points are highlighted in bold print.

Forgiveness is not forgetting. People who want to forget all that was done to them will find they cannot do it. When God says, He will remember our sins no more, He is saying that He will not use the past against us. Forgetting is a long term by-product of forgiveness, but it is never a means towards it. Don't put off forgiving those who have hurt you, hoping the pain will go away. Once you choose to forgive someone, *then* Christ will begin to heal your wounds. We don't heal in order to forgive; we forgive in order to heal.

Forgiveness is a choice, a decision of the will. Since God requires you to forgive, it is something you can do. Some people hold on to their anger as a means of protecting themselves against further abuse, but all they are doing is hurting themselves. Others want revenge. The Bible teaches, "'It is mine to avenge; I will repay,' says the Lord" (Romans 12:19, NIV). Let God deal with the person. Let him or her off your hook because as long as you refuse to forgive someone, you are still hooked to that person. You are still chained to your past, bound up in your bitterness. By forgiving, you let the other person off your hook, but he or she is not off God's hook. You must trust that God will deal with the person justly and fairly, something you simply cannot do.

But you don't know how much this person hurt me! No other human really knows another person's pain, but Jesus does, and instructs us to forgive others for our own sake. Until you let go of your bitterness, and hate, the person is still hurting you. Nobody can fix your past, but you can be free from it. What you gain by forgiving is freedom from your past and those who have abused you. Forgiveness is to set a captive free and then realize you we were the captive.

Forgiveness is agreeing to live with the consequences of another person's sin. We are all living with the consequences of someone else's sin. The only choice is to do so in the *bondage of bitterness* or in the *freedom of* *forgiveness.* But where is the justice? The cross makes forgiveness legally and morally right. Jesus died, once, for all our sins. We are to forgive as Christ has forgiven us. He did that by taking upon Himself the consequences of our sins. God "made Him who knew no sin to be sin on our behalf, that we might become the righteousness of God in Him" (2 Corinthians 5:21). Do not wait for the other person to ask for your forgiveness. Remember, Jesus did not wait for those who were crucifying Him to apologize before He forgave them. Even while they mocked and jeered at Him, He prayed, "Father, forgive them; for they do not know what they are doing" (Luke 23:34).

Forgive from your heart. Allow God to bring to the surface the painful memories and acknowledge how you feel towards those who've hurt you. If your forgiveness doesn't touch the emotional core of your life, it will be incomplete. Too often we're afraid of the pain so we bury our emotions deep down inside us. Let God bring them to the surface so He can begin to heal those damaged emotions.

Forgiveness is choosing not to hold someone's sin against him or her any more. It is common for bitter people to bring up past offenses with those who have hurt them. They want them to feel as bad as they do! But we must let go of the past and choose to reject any thought of revenge. This doesn't mean you continue to put up with the abuse. God does not tolerate sin and neither should you. You will need to set up scriptural boundaries that put a stop to further abuse. Take a stand against sin while continuing to exercise grace and forgiveness towards those who hurt you. If you need help setting scriptural boundaries to protect yourself from further abuse, talk to a trusted friend, counsellor, or discipler.

Don't wait until you feel like forgiving. You will never get there. Make the hard choice to forgive even if you don't feel like it. Once you choose to forgive, Satan will lose his hold on you, and God will begin to heal your damaged emotions.

Start with the first person on your list, and make the choice to forgive him or her for every painful memory that comes to your mind. Stay with that individual until you are sure you have dealt with all the remembered pain. Then work your way down the list in the same way.

As you begin forgiving people, God may bring to your mind painful memories you've totally forgotten. Let Him do this even if it hurts. God is surfacing those painful memories so you can face them once for all time and let them go. Don't excuse the offender's behaviour, even if it is someone you are really close to.

Don't say, "Lord, please help me to forgive." He is already helping you and will be with you all the way through the process. Don't say, "Lord, I want to forgive," because that bypasses the hard choice we have to make. Say, "Lord, I choose to forgive these people and what they did to me."

For every painful memory that God reveals for each person on your list, pray as follows:

> **Dear Heavenly Father, I choose to forgive** (name the person) **for** (what they did or failed to do), **because it made me feel** (share the painful feelings, for example, rejected, dirty, worthless, or inferior).

After you have forgiven every person for every painful memory, then pray as follows:

> **Lord Jesus, I choose not to hold on to my resentment. I relinquish my right to seek revenge and ask you to heal my damaged emotions. Thank You for setting me free from the bondage of my bitterness. I now ask You to bless those who have hurt me. In Jesus' name I pray. Amen.**

Note: During this step God may have brought to your mind people that you have knowingly or unknowingly wounded. See appendix B for steps in seeking the forgiveness of others.

CHOOSING THE TRUTH ABOUT YOUR HEAVENLY FATHER

Before we came to Christ, thoughts were raised up in our minds against a true knowledge of God (2 Corinthians 10:3–5). What we believe about our earthly fathers often distorts what we believe about our heavenly Father. Even as believers we can harbour resentments towards God and that will hinder our walk with Him. We should have a healthy fear of God (awe of His holiness, power, and presence), but we fear no punishment from Him. Romans 8:15 reads, "For you have not received a spirit of slavery leading to fear again, but you have received a spirit of adoption as sons by which we cry out, 'Abba! Father!'" Renew your mind with the true knowledge of God by reading the following list **aloud**:

I renounce the lie that You, Father God, are distant and uninterested in me.
I choose to believe the truth that You, Father God, are always personally present with me, have plans to give me a hope and a future, and have prepared works in advance specifically for me to do. (Psalm139:1–18; Matthew 28:20, Jeremiah 29:11, Ephesians 2:10)

I renounce the lie that You, Father God, are insensitive and don't know me or care for me.
I choose to believe the truth that You, Father God, are kind and compassionate and know every single thing about me. (Psalm 103:8–14; 1 John 3:1–3; Hebrews 4:12–13)

I renounce the lie that You, Father God, are stern and have placed unrealistic expectations on me.
I choose to believe the truth that You, Father God, have accepted me and are joyfully supportive of me. (Romans 5:8–11; 15:17)

I renounce the lie that You, Father God, are passive and cold towards me.
I choose to believe the truth that You, Father God, are warm and affectionate towards me. (Isaiah 40:11; Hosea 11:3–4)

I renounce the lie that You, Father God, are absent or too busy for me.
I choose to believe the truth that You, Father God, are always present and eager to be with me and enable me to be all that You created me to be. (Philippians 1:6; Hebrews 13:5)

I renounce the lie that You, Father God, are impatient or angry with me, or have rejected me.
I choose to believe the truth that You, Father God, are patient and slow to anger, and that when You discipline me, it is a proof of Your love, and not rejection. (Exodus 34:6; Romans 2:4; Hebrews 12:5–11)

I renounce the lie that You, Father God, have been mean, cruel, or abusive to me.
I choose to believe the truth that Satan is mean, cruel, and abusive, but You, Father God, are loving, gentle, and protective. (Psalm 18:2; Matthew 11:28–30; Ephesians 6:10–18)

I renounce the lie that You, Father God, are denying me the pleasures of life.
I choose to believe the truth that You, Father God, are the author of life and will lead me into love, joy, and peace when I choose to be filled with Your Spirit. (Lamentations 3:22–23; Galatians 5: 22–24)

I renounce the lie that You, Father God, are trying to control and manipulate me.
I choose to believe the truth that You, Father God, have set me free, and give me the freedom to make choices and grow in Your grace. (Galatians 5:1; Hebrews 4:15–16)

I renounce the lie that You, Father God, have condemned me, and no longer forgive me.
I choose to believe the truth that You, Father God, have forgiven all my sins and will never use them against me in the future. (Jeremiah 31:31–34; Romans 8:1)

I renounce the lie that You, Father God, reject me when I fail to live a perfect or sinless life.
I choose to believe the truth that You, Father God are patient towards me and cleanse me when I fail. (Proverbs 24:16; 1 John 1:7–2:2)

I AM THE APPLE OF YOUR EYE! (Deuteronomy 32:9–10)

STEP FOUR
REBELLION VERSUS SUBMISSION

We live in rebellious times. Many people sit in judgment of those in authority over them, and they submit only when it is convenient, or because they fear being caught. The Bible instructs us to pray for those in authority over us (1 Timothy 2:1–2), and submit to governing authorities (Romans 13:1–7). Rebelling against God and His established authority leaves us spiritually vulnerable. The only time God permits us to disobey earthly leaders is when they require us to do something morally wrong, or attempt to rule outside the realm of their authority. To have a submissive spirit and servant's heart, pray the following prayer:

> **Dear Heavenly Father, You have said that rebellion is like the sin of witchcraft and arrogance like the evil of idolatry** [see 1 Samuel 15:23]. **I know that I have not always been submissive, but instead have rebelled in my heart against You and against those You have placed in authority over me in attitude and in action. Please show me all the ways I have been rebellious. I choose now to adopt a submissive spirit and a servant's heart. In Jesus' name I pray. Amen.**

It is an act of faith to trust God to work in our lives through leaders who are something less than perfect, but that is what God is asking us to do. Should those in positions of leadership or power abuse their authority and break the laws designed to protect innocent people, you need to seek help from a higher authority. Many governments require certain types of abuse to be reported to a governmental agency. If that is your situation, we urge you to get the help you need immediately. Don't, however, assume that someone in authority is violating God's Word just because he or she is telling you to do something you don't like. God has set up specific lines of authority to protect us and give order to society. It is the position of authority that we respect. Without governing authorities every society would be chaos. From the list below, allow God to show you any specific ways you have been rebellious and use the prayer that follows to confess those sins He brings to mind.

- ❑ Civil government (including traffic laws, tax laws, attitude towards government officials), (Romans 13:1–7; 1 Timothy 2:1–4; 1 Peter 2:13–17)

- ❑ Parents, step-parents, or legal guardians (Ephesians 6:1–3)

- ❑ Teachers, coaches, school officials (Romans 13:1–4)

- ❑ Employers (past and present), (1 Peter 2:18–23)

- ❑ Husband (1 Peter 3:1–4) or wife (Ephesians 5:21; 1 Peter 3:7)
  [**Note to husbands:** Ask the Lord if your lack of love for your wife could be fostering a rebellious spirit within her. If so, confess that as a violation of Ephesians 5:22–33.]

- ❑ Church leaders (Hebrews 13:7)

- ❑ God (Daniel 9:5,9)

For each way in which the Spirit of God brings to your mind that you have been rebellious, use the following prayer to specifically confess that sin:

> **Heavenly Father, I confess that I have been rebellious towards** (name or position) **by** (specifically confess what you did or did not do). **Thank You for Your forgiveness. I choose to be submissive and obedient to Your Word. In Jesus' name I pray. Amen.**

STEP FIVE
PRIDE VERSUS HUMILITY

Pride comes before a fall, but God gives grace to the humble (James 4:6; 1 Peter 5:1–10). Humility is confidence properly placed in God, and we are instructed to, "put no confidence in the flesh" (Philippians 3:3). We are to be, "strong in the Lord and in the strength of His might" (Ephesians 6:10, KJV). Proverbs 3:5–7 urges us to trust in the Lord with all our hearts and to not lean on our own understanding. Use the following prayer to ask for God's guidance:

> Dear Heavenly Father, You have said that pride goes before destruction and an arrogant spirit before stumbling. I confess that I have focused on my own needs and desires and not those of others. I have not always denied myself, picked up my cross daily and followed You. I have relied on my own strength and resources instead of resting in Yours. I have placed my will before Yours and centred my life around myself instead of You. I confess my pride and selfishness and pray that all ground gained in my life by the enemies of the Lord Jesus Christ would be cancelled as I repent and overcome these sinful flesh patterns. I choose to rely upon the Holy Spirit's power and guidance so that I will do nothing from selfishness or empty conceit. With humility of mind, I choose to regard others as more important than myself. I acknowledge You as my Lord, and confess that apart from You I can do nothing of lasting significance. Please examine my heart and show me the specific ways I have lived my life in pride. In the gentle and humble name of Jesus I pray. Amen. (See Proverbs 16:18; Matthew 6:33; 16:24; Romans 12:10; Philippians 2:3.)

Pray through the list below and use the prayer following to confess any sins of pride the Lord brings to mind.

- ❑ Having a stronger desire to do my will than God's will
- ❑ Leaning too much on my own understanding and experience rather than seeking God's guidance through prayer and His Word
- ❑ Relying on my own strengths and resources instead of depending on the power of the Holy Spirit
- ❑ Being more concerned about controlling others than in developing self-control
- ❑ Being too busy doing "important" and selfish things rather than seeking and doing God's will
- ❑ Having a tendency to think that I have no needs
- ❑ Finding it hard to admit when I am wrong
- ❑ Being more concerned about pleasing people than pleasing God
- ❑ Being overly concerned about getting the credit I feel I deserve
- ❑ Thinking I am more humble, spiritual, religious, or devoted than others
- ❑ Being driven to obtain recognition by attaining degrees, titles, and positions
- ❑ Often feeling that my needs are more important than another person's needs
- ❑ Considering myself better than others because of my academic, artistic, athletic, or other abilities and accomplishments
- ❑ Not waiting on God
- ❑ Other ways I have thought more highly of myself than I should

For each of the above areas that has been true in your life, pray:

> Dear Heavenly Father, I agree I have been proud by (name what you selected above). Thank You for Your forgiveness. I choose to humble myself before You and others. I choose to place all my confidence in You and put no confidence in my flesh. In Jesus' name I pray. Amen.

STEP SIX
BONDAGE VERSUS FREEDOM

Many times we feel trapped in a vicious cycle of "sin confess, sin confess" that never seems to end but God's promises say, "God is faithful, and will not let you be tempted beyond your ability, but with the temptation will also provide the way of escape" (1 Corinthians 10:13), and "Submit therefore to God. Resist the devil and he will flee from you" (James 4:7). If you did not choose the way of escape and sinned, then you should confess that to God, ask Him to fill you will His Holy Spirit, resist the devil by putting on the full armour of God (see Ephesians 6:10–20) and he will flee from you.

Sin that has become a habit often may require help from a trusted brother or sister in Christ. James 5:16 says, "Confess your sins to one another, and pray for one another, so that you may be healed. The effective prayer of a righteous man can accomplish much." Sometimes the assurance of 1 John 1:9 is enough: "If we confess our sins, He is faithful and righteous to forgive us our sins and to cleanse us from all unrighteousness."

Remember, confession is not saying, "I'm sorry." It is openly admitting, "I did it." Whether you need help from other people or just the accountability of walking in the light before God, pray the following prayer:

> **Dear Heavenly Father, You have told me to put on the Lord Jesus Christ and make no provision for the flesh in regard to its lust. I confess that I have given in to fleshly lusts that wage war against my soul. I thank You that in Christ my sins are already forgiven, but I have broken Your holy law and I have allowed sin to wage war in my body. I come to You now to confess and renounce these sins of the flesh so that I might be cleansed and set free from the bondage of sin. Please reveal to my mind all the sins of the flesh I have committed and the ways I have grieved the Holy Spirit. In Jesus' holy name, I pray. Amen.** (See Romans 6:12–13; 13:14; 2 Corinthians 4:2; James 4:1; 1 Peter 2:11; 5:8)

The following list contains many sins of the flesh but a prayerful examination of Mark 7:20–23, Galatians 5:19–21, Ephesians 4:25–31 and other passages will help you to be even more thorough. Look over the list below and ask the Holy Spirit to bring to your mind the sins you need to confess. He may reveal others to you as well. For each sin the Lord shows you, pray a prayer of confession from your heart. There is a sample prayer following the list.

Note: Sexual sins, marriage and divorce issues, gender identity, abortion, suicidal tendencies, perfectionism, eating disorders, substance abuse, gambling and bigotry will be dealt with later in this step.

❑ Stealing	❑ Swearing	❑ Cheating
❑ Quarreling/fighting	❑ Apathy/laziness	❑ Avoiding responsibility
❑ Jealousy/envy	❑ Lying	❑ Greed/materialism
❑ Complaining/criticism	❑ Hatred	❑ Others: _____
❑ Sarcasm	❑ Anger	
❑ Gossip/slander	❑ Drunkenness	

> **Dear Heavenly Father, I confess that I have sinned against You by** (name the sins). **Thank You for Your forgiveness and cleansing. I now turn away from these expressions of sin and turn to You, Lord. Fill me with Your Holy Spirit so that I will not carry out the desires of the flesh. In Jesus' name I pray. Amen.**

RESOLVING SEXUAL SIN

It is our responsibility not to allow sin to reign (rule) in our physical bodies. To avoid that we must not use our bodies or another person's body as an instrument of unrighteousness (see Romans 6:12–13). Sexual immorality is not only a sin against God, but is a sin against your body, the temple of the Holy Spirit (1 Corinthians 6:18–19). Sex was intended by God to be the means for procreation and for the pleasure of a husband and wife. When marriage is consummated they become one flesh. If we sexually join our bodies to another person outside of marriage we also become "one flesh" (1 Corinthians 6:16), which creates a spiritual bond between two people leading to spiritual bondage whether it is heterosexual or homosexual. Sexual relations between people of the same sex are explicitly forbidden by God, but so is sex with someone of the opposite sex who is not your spouse. To find freedom from sexual bondage, begin by praying the following prayer:

> **Dear Heavenly Father, I have allowed sin to reign in my mortal body. I ask You to bring to my mind every sexual use of my body as an instrument of unrighteousness so that I can renounce these sexual sins and break those sinful bondages. In Jesus' name I pray. Amen.**

As the Lord brings to your mind every immoral sexual use of your body, whether it was done to you (rape, incest, sexual molestation) or willingly by you (pornography, masturbation, sexual immorality), renounce every experience as follows:

> **Dear Heavenly Father, I renounce** (name the sexual experience) **with** (name). **I ask You to break that sinful bond with** (name) **spiritually, physically, and emotionally** (repeat for each experience). **In Jesus' name I pray. Amen.**

If you have used pornography, say the following prayer:

> **Dear Heavenly Father, I confess that I have looked at sexually suggestive and pornographic material for the purpose of stimulating myself sexually. I have attempted to satisfy my lustful desires and polluted my body, soul, and spirit. Thank You for cleansing me and for Your forgiveness. I renounce any satanic bonds I have allowed in my life through the unrighteous use of my body and mind. Lord, I commit myself to destroy any objects in my possession that I have used for sexual stimulation, and to turn away from all media that are associated with my sexual sin. I commit myself to the renewing of my mind and to think pure thoughts. Fill me with your Holy Spirit that I may not carry out the desires of the flesh. In Jesus' name I pray. Amen.**

After you have finished, commit your body to God by praying:

> **Dear Heavenly Father, I renounce all these uses of my body as an instrument of unrighteousness, and I admit to any wilful participation. I choose to present my physical body to You as an instrument of righteousness, a living and holy sacrifice, acceptable to You. I choose to reserve the sexual use of my body for marriage only. I reject the devil's lie that my body is not clean or that it is dirty or in any way unacceptable to You as a result of my past sexual experiences. Lord, thank You that You have cleansed and forgiven me and that You love and accept me just the way I am. Therefore, I choose now to accept myself and my body as clean in Your eyes. In Jesus' name I pray. Amen.**

The following prayers will enhance your growth process and help you make critical decisions. On their own they are unlikely to bring complete resolution or recovery but are an excellent starting point. You will then need to work on renewing your mind. Please don't hesitate to seek godly counsel for additional help when needed.

Marriage

Dear Heavenly Father, I choose to believe that You created us male and female, and that marriage is a spiritual bond between one man and one woman who become one in Christ. I believe that bond can only be broken by death, adultery or desertion by an unbelieving spouse. I choose to stay committed to my vows and to remain faithful to my spouse until physical death separates us. Give me the grace to be the spouse You created me to be, and enable me to love and respect my partner in marriage. I will seek to change only myself and accept my spouse as You have accepted me. Teach me how to speak the truth in love, to be merciful as You have been merciful to me, and to forgive as You have forgiven me. In Jesus' name I pray. Amen.

Divorce

Dear Heavenly Father, I have not been the spouse You created me to be, and I deeply regret that my marriage has failed. I choose to believe that You still love and accept me. I choose to believe that I am still Your child, and that Your desire for me is that I continue serving You and others in Your Kingdom. Give me the grace to overcome the disappointment and the emotional scars that I carry, and I ask the same for my ex-spouse. I choose to forgive him/her and I choose to forgive myself for all the ways I contributed to the divorce. Enable me to learn from my mistakes and guide me so that I don't repeat the same old flesh patterns. I choose to believe the truth that I am still accepted, secure, and significant in Christ. Please guide me to healthy relationships in Your Church, and keep me from seeking a marriage on the rebound. I trust You to supply all my needs in the future, and I commit myself to follow You. In Jesus' name I pray. Amen.

Gender Identity

Dear Heavenly Father, I choose to believe that You have created all humanity to be either male or female (Genesis 1:27) and commanded us to maintain a distinction between the two genders (Deuteronomy 22:5; Romans 1:24–29). I confess that I have been influenced by the social pressures of this fallen world and the lies of Satan to question my biological gender identity and that of others. I renounce all the accusations and lies of Satan that would seek to convince me that I am somebody other than who You created me to be. I choose to believe and accept my biological gender identity, and pray that You would heal my damaged emotions and enable me to be transformed by the renewing of my mind. I take up the full armour of God (Ephesians 6:13) and the shield of faith to extinguish all the temptations and accusation of the evil one (Ephesians 6:16). I renounce any identities and labels that derive from my old nature, and I choose to believe that I am a new creation in Christ. In the Wonderful name of Jesus, I pray. Amen.

Abortion

Dear Heavenly Father, I confess that I was not a proper guardian and keeper of the life You entrusted to me, and I confess that I have sinned. Thank You that because of Your forgiveness, I can forgive myself. I commit the child to You for all eternity, and believe that he or she is in Your caring hands. In Jesus' name I pray. Amen.

Suicidal Tendencies

Dear Heavenly Father, I renounce all suicidal thoughts and any attempts I've made to take my own life or in any way injure myself. I renounce the lie that life is hopeless and that I can find peace and freedom by taking my own life. Satan is a thief and comes to steal, kill, and destroy. I choose to remain alive in Christ who said He came to give me life and give it abundantly. Thank You for Your forgiveness that allows me to forgive myself. I choose to believe that there is always hope in Christ and that my Heavenly Father loves me. In Jesus' name, I pray. Amen.

Substance Abuse

Dear Heavenly Father, I confess that I have misused substances (alcohol, tobacco, food, prescription, or street drugs) for the purpose of pleasure, to escape reality, or to cope with difficult problems. I confess that I have abused my body and programmed my mind in harmful ways. I have quenched the Holy Spirit as well. Thank You for Your forgiveness. I renounce any satanic connection or influence in my life through my misuse of food or chemicals. I cast my anxieties onto Christ who loves me. I commit myself to yield no longer to substance abuse, but instead I choose to allow the Holy Spirit to direct and empower me. In Jesus' name I pray. Amen.

Eating Disorders or Self Mutilation

Dear Heavenly Father, I renounce the lie that my value as a person is dependent upon my appearance or performance. I renounce cutting or abusing myself, vomiting, using laxatives or starving myself as a means of being in control, altering my appearance, or trying to cleanse myself of evil. I announce that only the blood of the Lord Jesus Christ cleanses me from sin. I realize I have been bought with a price and my body, the temple of the Holy Spirit, belongs to God. Therefore, I choose to glorify God in my body. I renounce the lie that I am evil or that any part of my body is evil. Thank You that You accept me just the way I am in Christ. In Jesus' name I pray. Amen.

Drivenness and Perfectionism

Dear Heavenly Father, I renounce the lie that my sense of worth is dependent upon my ability to perform. I announce the truth that my identity and sense of worth are found in who I am as Your child. I renounce seeking the approval and acceptance of other people for my affirmation, and I choose to believe he truth that I am already approved and accepted in Christ, because of His death and resurrection for me. I choose to believe the truth that I have been saved, not by deeds done in righteousness, but according to Your mercy. I choose to believe that I am no longer under the curse of the law, because Christ became a curse for me. I receive the free gift of life in Christ and choose to abide in Him. I renounce striving for perfection by living under the law. By Your grace, Heavenly Father, I choose from this day forward to walk by faith in the power of Your Holy Spirit according to what You have said is true. In Jesus' name I pray. Amen.

Gambling

Dear Heavenly Father, I confess that I have been a poor steward of the financial resources that have been in my possession. I have gambled away my future chasing a false god. I have not been content with food and clothing, and the love of money has driven me to behave irrationally and sinfully. I renounce making provision for my flesh in regard to this lust. I commit myself to stay away from all gambling casinos, gambling websites, bookmakers, and lottery sales. I choose to believe that I am alive in Christ and dead to sin. Fill me with Your Holy Spirit so that I don't carry out the desires of the flesh. Show me the way of escape when I am tempted to return to my addictive behaviours. I stand against all of Satan's accusations, temptations, and deceptions by putting on the armour of God and standing firm in my faith. I choose to believe that You will meet all my needs according to Your riches in glory. In Jesus' name I pray. Amen.

Bigotry

Dear Heavenly Father, You have created all humanity in Your image. I confess that I have judged others by the colour of their skin, their national origin, their social or economic status, their cultural differences, or their sexual orientation. I renounce racism, elitism, and sexism. I choose to believe "There is neither Jew nor Greek, there is neither slave nor free, there is neither male nor female, for you are all one in Christ" (Galatians 3:28). Please show me the roots of my own bigotry that I may confess it and be cleansed from such defilement. I pledge myself "to walk in a manner worthy of the calling to which I have been called, with humility and gentleness, with patience, bearing with one another in love, eager to maintain the unity of the Spirit in the bond of peace" (Ephesians 4:1–3, ESV). In Jesus' name I pray. Amen.

Fear and Anxiety

See appendices C and D for a comprehensive process for overcoming fear and anxiety issues that are rampant around the world.

STEP SEVEN
CURSES VERSUS BLESSINGS

The Bible declares that the iniquities of one generation can be visited on to the third and fourth generations of those who hate God, but God's blessings will be poured out on thousands of generations of those who love and obey Him (Exodus 20:4–6). The iniquities of one generation can adversely affect future ones unless those sins are renounced, and your new spiritual heritage in Christ is claimed. This cycle of abuse and all negative influences can be stopped through genuine repentance. You are not guilty of your ancestor's sins, but because of their sins you have been affected by their influence. Jesus said that after we have been fully trained we will be like our teachers (Luke 6:40), and Peter wrote that you were redeemed "from your futile way of life inherited from your forefathers" (1 Peter 1:18). Ask the Lord to reveal your ancestral sins and then renounce them as follows:

Dear Heavenly Father, please reveal to my mind all the sins of my ancestors that have been passed down through family lines. Since I am a new creation in Christ, I want to experience my freedom from those influences and walk in my new identity as a child of God. In Jesus' name I pray. Amen.

Listen carefully to what the Holy Spirit may reveal, and list anything that comes to your mind. God may reveal cult and occultic religious practices of your ancestors that you were not aware of. Also, every family has a history of issues such as mental illnesses, sicknesses, divorce, sexual sins, anger, depression, fear, violence, and abuse.

When nothing else comes to mind, conclude with:

Lord, I renounce (name all the family sins that God brings to your mind).

We cannot passively take our place in Christ, we must actively and intentionally choose to submit to God, resist the devil, and then he will flee from us. Verbally complete this final step with the following declaration and prayer:

DECLARATION

I here and now reject and disown all the sins of my ancestors. As one who has been delivered from the domain of darkness and transferred into the kingdom of God's Son, I declare myself to be free from those harmful influences. I am no longer "in Adam." I am now alive "in Christ." Therefore I am the recipient of the blessings of God upon my life as I choose to love and obey Him. As one who has been crucified and raised with Christ and who sits with Him in heavenly places, I renounce any and all satanic attacks and assignments directed against me and my ministry. Every curse placed on me was broken when Christ became a curse for me by dying on the cross (Galatians 3:13). I reject any and every way in which Satan may claim ownership of me. I belong to the Lord Jesus Christ who purchased me with His own precious blood. I declare myself to be fully and eternally signed over and committed to the Lord Jesus Christ. Therefore, having submitted to God, I now by His authority resist the devil, and I command every spiritual enemy of the Lord Jesus Christ to leave my presence. I put on the armour of God and I stand against Satan's temptations, accusations, and deceptions. From this day forward I will seek to do only the will of my Heavenly Father.

PRAYER

Dear Heavenly Father, I come to You as Your child, bought out of slavery to sin by the blood of the Lord Jesus Christ. You are the Lord of the universe and the Lord of my life. I submit my body to You as a living and holy sacrifice. May You be glorified through my life and body. I now ask You to fill me with Your Holy Spirit. I commit myself to the renewing of my mind in order that I may prove that Your will is good, acceptable, and perfect for me. I desire nothing more than to be like You. I pray, believe, and do all this in the wonderful name of Jesus, my Lord and Saviour. Amen.

INCOMPLETE RESOLUTION?

After you have completed the *Steps*, close your eyes and sit silently for a minute or two. Is it quiet in your mind? Most will sense the peace of God and a clear mind. A small percentage of believers don't, and usually they know that there is still some unfinished business with God. If you believe that you have been totally honest with God, and processed all the *Steps* to the best of your ability, then ask God as follows:

Dear Heavenly Father, I earnestly desire Your presence, and I am asking You to reveal to my mind what is keeping me from experiencing that. I ask that You take me back to times of trauma in my life and show me the lies that I have believed. I pray that You will grant me the repentance that leads to a knowledge of the truth that will set me free. I humbly ask that You would heal my damaged emotions. In Jesus' name I pray. Amen.

Don't spend your time trying to figure out what is wrong with you if nothing new surfaces. You are only responsible to deal with what you know. Instead, commit yourself to find out what is right about you, that is who you are in Christ. Some believers can sense a new found freedom and then days or weeks later begin to struggle again. Chances are God is revealing some more of your past that needs to be dealt with. God reveals one layer at a time for those who have experienced severe trauma. Trying to deal with every abuse in one setting may be too overwhelming for some. If we show ourselves faithful in little things, God will put us in charge of bigger things.

The following page shows clearly what is true about you!

I renounce the lie that I am rejected, unloved, or shameful. In Christ I am accepted.

God says:

> I am God's child (John 1:12)
> I am Christ's friend (John 15:5)
> I have been justified (Romans 5:1)
> I am united with the Lord and I am one spirit with Him (1 Corinthians 6:17)
> I have been bought with a price: I belong to God (1 Corinthians 6:19–20)
> I am a member of Christ's body (1 Corinthians 12:27)
> I am a saint, a holy one (Ephesians 1:1)
> I have been adopted as God's child (Ephesians 1:5)
> I have direct access to God through the Holy Spirit (Ephesians 2:18)
> I have been redeemed and forgiven of all my sins (Colossians 1:14)
> I am complete in Christ (Colossians 2:10)

I renounce the lie that I am guilty, unprotected, alone, or abandoned. In Christ I am secure.

God says:

> I am free from condemnation (Romans 8:1–2)
> I am assured that all things work together for good (Romans 8:28)
> I am free from any condemning charges against me (Romans 8:31–34)
> I cannot be separated from the love of God (Romans 8:35–39)
> I have been established, anointed, and sealed by God (2 Corinthians 1:21–22)
> I am confident that the good work God has begun in me will be perfected (Philippians 1:6)
> I am a citizen of heaven (Philippians 3:20)
> I am hidden with Christ in God (Colossians 3:3)
> I have not been given a spirit of fear, but of power, love, and self-control (2 Timothy 1:7)
> I can find grace and mercy to help in time of need (Hebrews 4:16)
> I am born of God and the evil one cannot touch me (1 John 5:18)

I renounce the lie that I am worthless, inadequate, helpless, or hopeless. In Christ I am significant.

God says:

> I am the salt of the earth and the light of the world (Matthew 5:13–14)
> I am a branch of the true vine, Jesus, a channel of His life (John 15:1,5)
> I have been chosen and appointed by God to bear fruit (John 15:16)
> I am a personal, Spirit-empowered witness of Christ's (Acts 1:8)
> I am a temple of God (1 Corinthians 3:16)
> I am a minister of reconciliation for God (2 Corinthians 5:17–21)
> I am a fellow worker with God (2 Corinthians 6:1)
> I am seated with Christ in the heavenly realms (Ephesians 2:6)
> I am God's workmanship, created for good works (Ephesians 2:10)
> I may approach God with freedom and confidence (Ephesians 3:12)
> I can do all things through Christ who strengthens me! (Philippians 4:13)

> I am not the great "I Am," but by the grace of God I am what I am. (See Exodus 3:14; John 8:24, 28, 58; 1 Corinthians 15:10.)

THE STEPS TO FREEDOM IN CHRIST

It is exciting to experience your freedom in Christ, but what you have gained must be maintained. You have won an important battle, but the war goes on. To maintain your freedom in Christ and grow as a disciple of Jesus in the grace of God, you must continue renewing your mind to the truth of God's word. If you become aware of lies that you have believed, renounce them and choose the truth. If more painful memories surface, then forgive those who hurt you and renounce any sinful part you played. Many people choose to go through the *Steps to Freedom in Christ* again on their own to make sure they have dealt with all their issues. Often new issues will surface. The process can assist you in a regular "house cleaning."

It is not uncommon after going through the *Steps* for people to have thoughts like: *Nothing has really changed*; *You're the same person you always were*; or *It didn't work*. In most cases you should just ignore it. We are not called to dispel the darkness, we are called to turn on the light. You don't get rid of negative thoughts by rebuking every one, you get rid of them by repenting and choosing the truth.

In the introduction you were encouraged to write down any false beliefs and lies that surfaced during the *Steps*. For the next forty days verbally work through that list saying: *I renounce (the lies you have believed)*, and *I announce the truth that (what you have chosen to believe is true based on God's Word)*.

I encourage you to read *Victory Over the Darkness* and *The Bondage Breaker* if you haven't already done so or to go through *The Freedom In Christ Course*. The 21-day devotional, *Walking in Freedom*, was written for those who have gone through the *Steps*. To continue growing in the grace of God I suggest the following:

1. Get rid of or destroy any cult or occult objects in your home. (See Acts 19:18–20.)
2. Be part of a church where God's truth is taught with kindness and grace and get involved in a small group where you can be honest and real.
3. Read and meditate on the truth of God's Word each day.
4. Don't let your mind be passive, especially concerning what you watch and listen to (for example, internet, music, TV). Actively take every thought captive to the obedience of Christ.
5. Be a good steward of your health and develop a godly lifestyle of rest, exercise, and proper diet.
6. Say the following daily prayer for the next forty days and the others prayers as needed.

DAILY PRAYER AND DECLARATION

Dear Heavenly Father, I praise You and honour You as my Lord and Saviour. You are in control of all things. I thank You that You are always with me and will never leave me nor forsake me. You are the only all-powerful and only wise God. You are kind and loving in all Your ways. I love You and thank You that I am united with Jesus and spiritually alive in Him. I choose not to love the world or the things in the world, and I crucify the flesh and all its passions.

Thank You for the life I now have in Christ. I ask You to fill me with the Holy Spirit so I can be guided by You and not carry out the desires of the flesh. I declare my total dependence upon You and I take my stand against Satan and all his lying ways. I choose to believe the truth of God's Word despite what my feelings may say. I refuse to be discouraged; You are the God of all hope. Nothing is too difficult for You. I am confident that You will supply all my needs as I seek to live according to Your Word. I thank You that I can be content and live a responsible life through Christ who strengthens me.

I now take my stand against Satan and command him and all his evil spirits to depart from me. I choose to put on the full armour of God so I may be able to stand firm against all the devil's schemes. I submit my body as a living and holy sacrifice to You, and I choose to renew my mind by Your living Word. By so doing I will be able to prove that Your will is good, acceptable, and perfect for me. In the name of my Lord and Saviour, Jesus Christ, I pray. Amen.

BEDTIME PRAYER

Thank You, Lord, that You have brought me into Your family and have blessed me with every spiritual blessing in the heavenly places in Christ Jesus. Thank You for this time of renewal and refreshment through sleep. I accept it as one of Your blessings for Your children and I trust You to guard my mind and my body during my sleep.

As I have thought about You and Your truth during the day, I choose to let those good thoughts continue in my mind while I am asleep. I commit myself to You for Your protection against every attempt of Satan and his demons to attack me during sleep. Guard my mind from nightmares. I renounce all fear and cast every anxiety upon You. I commit myself to You as my rock, my fortress, and my strong tower. May Your peace be upon this place of rest. In the strong name of the Lord Jesus Christ I pray. Amen.

PRAYER FOR SPIRITUAL CLEANSING OF HOME/APARTMENT/ROOM

After removing and destroying all objects of false worship, pray this prayer aloud in every room:

Dear Heavenly Father, I acknowledge that You are the Lord of heaven and earth. In Your sovereign power and love, You have entrusted many things to me. Thank You for this place to live. I claim my home as a place of spiritual safety for me and my family and ask for Your protection from all the attacks of the enemy. As a child of God, raised up and seated with Christ in the heavenly places, I command every evil spirit claiming ground in this place, based on the activities of past or present occupants, including me and my family, to leave and never return. I renounce all demonic assignments directed against this place. I ask You, Heavenly Father, to post Your holy angels around this place to guard it from any and all attempts of the enemy to enter and disturb Your purposes for me and my family. I thank You, Lord, for doing this in the name of the Lord Jesus Christ. Amen.

PRAYER FOR LIVING IN A NON-CHRISTIAN ENVIRONMENT

After removing and destroying all objects of false worship from your possession, pray this aloud in the place where you live:

Thank You, Heavenly Father, for a place to live and to be renewed by sleep. I ask You to set aside my room (or portion of this room) as a place of spiritual safety for me. I renounce any allegiance given to false gods or spirits by other occupants. I renounce any claim to this room (space) by Satan based on the activities of past or present occupants, including me. On the basis of my position as a child of God and joint heir with Christ, who has all authority in heaven and on earth, I command all evil spirits to leave this place and never return. I ask You, Heavenly Father, to station Your holy angels to protect me while I live here. In Jesus' mighty name I pray. Amen.

APPENDIX A
RENOUNCING SATANIC WORSHIP

Satan is the god of this world, and there are Satanists who worship him in secret societies and ceremonies. They meet from midnight to three in the morning when a horde of demons are sent to terrorize, deceive, and destroy the defenceless. If any Christian has been suddenly awakened at 3:00 AM or emotionally overcome with a sense of terror they can immediately stop such attacks by submitting to God and resisting the devil in that order (James 4:7). The weapons of our warfare are not of the flesh, so physical attempts to stop the attack may prove futile. God knows our thoughts so we can always submit to Him inwardly, and instantly we will be freed up to call upon the name of the Lord and be saved. All you would have to say is, *Jesus*, but you would have to say it, which is why you need to submit to God first.

There are many victims who have been subjected to satanic ritual abuse. It is likely that they will develop alternate personalities to deal with the trauma. They are not in bondage to the trauma, they are in bondage to the lies they believe because of the trauma. Those lies are deeply embedded and need to be renounced so the truth can set them free. Satanic rituals counterfeit Christian worship. Such victims can start their recovery by renouncing satanic lies and assignments and announcing true Christian worship as follows:

I renounce ever signing my name over to Satan or having my name signed over to Satan.

I announce that my name is now written in the Lamb's book of life (Revelation 3:5; 20:15).

I renounce any ceremony in which I have been wed to Satan.

I announce that I am the bride of Christ (Ephesians 5:32; Revelation 19:7).

I renounce any and all covenants I made with Satan.

I announce that I am alive in Christ and under the new covenant of grace (2 Corinthians 3:6).

I renounce all satanic assignments for my life, including duties, marriage, and children.

I announce and commit myself to know and do only the will of God (Matthew 7:21–23).

I renounce all spirit guides assigned to me.

I accept only the leading of the Holy Spirit (1 John 4:1–6).

I renounce ever giving my blood in the service of Satan.

I trust only the blood of the Lord Jesus Christ to save me (Revelation 1:5).

I renounce ever eating flesh or drinking blood for satanic worship.

I acknowledge only the flesh and blood of the Lord Jesus Christ in Holy Communion (1 Corinthians 10:14–21).

I renounce all guardians and Satanist parents who were assigned to me.

I announce that God is my Father and the Holy Spirit is my guardian by whom I am sealed.

I renounce any baptism whereby I have been identified with Satan.

I announce that I have been baptised into Christ Jesus (1 Corinthians 12:13).

I renounce any and all sacrifices that were made on my behalf by which Satan may claim ownership of me.

I announce that only the sacrifice of Christ has any hold on me. I belong to Jesus.

Those who have been ritually abused will slowly recover memories, and when they surface there will always be something to renounce and someone to forgive. If you suspect previous satanic activity or have periods of memory loss use the renunciations to ascertain the problem's source.

APPENDIX B
SEEKING THE FORGIVENESS OF OTHERS

Jesus said, "So if you are offering your gift at the altar and there remember that your brother has something against you, leave your gift there before the altar and go. First be reconciled to your brother, and then come and offer your gift. Come to terms quickly with your accuser . . ." (Matthew 5:23–25a, ESV). If someone has hurt you, then go to God. You don't need to go to the offender to forgive them, and in many cases that would be inadvisable. Your need to forgive another is primarily an issue between you and God. However, if you have offended another, you must go to them and ask for their forgiveness and make amends when appropriate. The following are steps to seeking forgiveness:

1. Be certain about what you did that was wrong and why it was wrong.
2. Make sure you have forgiven them for whatever they have done to you.
3. Think through exactly how you will ask them to forgive you.
4. Be sure to state that what you did was wrong.
5. Be specific and admit that you did it.
6. Don't offer any excuses or try to defend yourself.
7. Place no blame on any others.
8. Don't expect that they will ask you for your forgiveness or let that be the reason for what you are doing.
9. Your confession should lead to the direct question: "Will you forgive me?"
10. Seek the right place and the right time, but the sooner the better.
11. Ask for forgiveness in person face-to-face.
12. Unless there is no other option, do not write a letter. It can be misunderstood, and others may see it who are not involved, and it could be used against you in a court case or otherwise.

"If possible, so far as it depends on you, live peacefully with all" (Romans 12:18), but it doesn't always depend on you. If the other person doesn't want to be reconciled, it won't happen. Reconciliation between two people requires repentance and forgiveness by both parties. Rarely is there one who is completely innocent. However, if you have forgiven the other person and genuinely asked their forgiveness, then you have done all God requires of you. Be at peace with God.

PRAYER FOR RESTORATION OF BROKEN RELATIONSHIPS

Dear Heavenly Father, I confess and repent of my sins against my neighbour (spouse, parents, children, relatives, friends, neighbours, or brothers and sisters in Christ). Thank You for Your forgiveness, and I forgive them for what they have done to me and I choose not to hold it against them in the future. I ask that You bless them and enable them to live with the consequences of my sin against them. I pray that You would heal the wounds from the sins I have inflicted on them. I ask the same for myself that I may be set free from the consequences of their sin or that You would give me the grace to live with the consequences without bitterness. I pray that You would heal my wounds and set me free so that I can live in peaceful co-existence with my neighbours, and with You. In Jesus' name I pray. Amen.

APPENDIX C
OVERCOMING FEAR

Fear is a God-given natural response when our physical or psychological safety is threatened. Fear always has an object, that is something or someone, and that object must be both *present* and *potent*, that is perceived to have some power over us. It ceases to be a fear object when only one of those attributes is eliminated.

Almost all fears are related to the fear of death, people, and Satan. Death is still *present* in that it is an imminent possibility, but it is no longer *potent* (see 1 Corinthians 15:54–55). The believer who dies physically is still alive spiritually and fully in God's presence. Paul wrote, "For me to live is Christ, and to die is gain" (Philippians 1:21).

People may threaten us when present, but Jesus said, "And do not fear those who kill the body but cannot kill the soul. Rather fear Him who can destroy both soul and body in hell" (Matthew 10:28, ESV). "And who is he who will harm you if you become followers of what is good? But even if you should suffer for righteousness' sake, you are blessed. And do not be afraid of their threats, nor be troubled. But sanctify the Lord God in your hearts" (1 Peter 3:13–15, NKJV).

Satan still roars around like a hungry lion, but he is disarmed (Colossians 2:15). People tend to fear Satan more than they fear God, which elevates him as a greater object of worship. The fear of God is the beginning of wisdom. He is the ultimate fear object because He is omnipresent and omnipotent. "Do not call conspiracy all that this people calls conspiracy, and do not fear what they fear, nor be in dread. But the Lord of hosts, Him you shall regard as holy. Let Him be your fear, and Him be your dread. And then He will become a sanctuary" (Isaiah 8:12–14).

Courage is not the absence of fear. Courage is choosing to live by faith and doing what is right in the face of perceived fear-objects. Behind every irrational fear is a lie, which must be identified. Ask the Lord to reveal to your mind the nature of your fears and the irrational lies that compel them as follows:

> **Dear Heavenly Father, I confess that I have allowed fear to control my life. Thank You for Your forgiveness. I choose to believe that You have not given me a spirit of fear, but of power, love, and self-control (2 Timothy 1:7). I renounce any spirit of fear operating in my life and ask You to reveal any and all controlling fears in my life and the lies behind them. I desire to live by faith according to what You have said is true in the power of the Holy Spirit. In Jesus' name I pray. Amen.**

- ❑ Fear of death
- ❑ Fear of never loving or being loved
- ❑ Fear of Satan
- ❑ Fear of embarrassment
- ❑ Fear of failure
- ❑ Fear of being victimized
- ❑ Fear of rejection by people
- ❑ Fear of marriage
- ❑ Fear of disapproval
- ❑ Fear of divorce
- ❑ Fear of becoming/being homosexual
- ❑ Fear of going crazy
- ❑ Fear of financial problems
- ❑ Fear of pain/illness

- ❏ Fear of never getting married
- ❏ Fear of the future
- ❏ Fear of the death of a loved one
- ❏ Fear of confrontation
- ❏ Fear of being a hopeless case
- ❏ Fear of specific individuals (list them):

_____

_____

_____

- ❏ Fear of losing my salvation
- ❏ Fear of not being loved by God
- ❏ Fear of having committed the unpardonable sin
- ❏ Other specific fears that come to mind now:

_____

_____

_____

Lord Jesus, I have allowed the fear of (name the fear object) **to control my life. I have believed** (state the lie). **I renounce all irrational fears and the lies behind them. I choose to live by faith, and acknowledge You as the only legitimate fear object in my life. In Jesus' name I pray. Amen.**

ANALYSE YOUR FEARS AND WORK OUT A RESPONSIBLE PLAN:

When did you first experience the fear, and what events preceded the first experience? Knowing such experiences can help you identity the basis for your fears. Fear is a powerful motivator for good and evil. "Therefore, knowing the fear of the Lord, we persuade others" (2 Corinthians 5:11, ESV).

How has fear:

1. Prevented you from doing what is responsible and right?
2. Compelled you to do something wrong and live irresponsibly?
3. Compromised your witness?

Once you have analysed your fear the next step is to work out a plan of responsible behaviour. This may require baby steps at first, and it may be helpful to invite a trusted friend to help you make the first step. Don't set yourself up for failure. Determine in advance what your reaction will be to any fear-object when confronted. Finally, commit yourself to carry out the plan. Do the thing you fear and the death of fear is certain. The key to any cure is commitment.

How to succeed

Nobody can keep you from having a successful life in God's kingdom if you follow these three principles:
1. Commit yourself to know God and His ways (Joshua 1:7–8).
2. Become the person God has created you to be (Philippians 3:12–14).
3. Be a good steward of the time, talent, and treasure that God has entrusted to you (1 Corinthians 4:1–2).

Note: For additional help read *Freedom From Fear*, Harvest House Publishers, 1999.

APPENDIX D
OVERCOMING ANXIETY

Anxiety is different from fear, because it doesn't have an object. People are anxious because they are uncertain about an outcome or don't know what is going to happen tomorrow. It is normal to be concerned about things we value; if we weren't it would show a lack of care. For some the intensity and regularity of anxiety is out of proportion to the actual problem. We have been admonished to cast all our anxieties upon Jesus (1 Peter 5:7).

The root word for anxiety in Scripture means "double-mindedness". The first step to become single-minded is to pray. "Be anxious for nothing, but in everything by prayer and supplication with thanksgiving let your requests be made known to God" (Philippians 4:6). Ask God to guide you through these steps to overcoming anxiety with the following prayer:

> **Dear Heavenly Father, I am Your child bought by the blood of the Lord Jesus Christ. I am completely dependent on You and I need You. I know that without Jesus I can't do anything. You know the thoughts and intentions in my heart and You know my situation from the beginning to the end. I feel as though I am double-minded, and I need Your peace to guard my heart and my mind. I humble myself before You and choose to trust You to exalt me at the right time in any way You choose. I trust You to meet all my needs according to Your riches in glory in Christ Jesus, and to guide me into all truth. Please guide me so that I can fulfil my calling to live a responsible life by faith in the power of Your Holy Spirit. "Search me, O God, and know my heart; try me and know my thoughts; and see if there be any hurtful way in me, and lead me in the everlasting way" (Psalm 139: 23, 24). In Jesus' precious name. Amen.**

RESOLVE ANY PERSONAL AND SPIRITUAL CONFLICTS

The purpose of the *Steps to Freedom in Christ* is to help you submit to God and resist the devil through repentance and faith in God. Then you will have "the peace of God which transcends all understanding, [that] will guard your hearts and your minds through Christ Jesus" (Philippians 4:7, NKJV). Repentance means a change of mind. Worrisome people struggle with anxious thoughts. Since "The Spirit clearly says that in later times some will abandon the faith and follow deceiving spirits and things taught by demons" (1 Timothy 4:1, NIV) it is imperative that we resist the devil and put on the armour of God. If you pay attention to a deceiving spirit you will be a double-minded person.

STATE THE PROBLEM

A problem well-stated is half-solved. When people are anxious they can't see the forest for the trees so start by putting the problem in perspective: *Will it matter for eternity?* Being overly anxious is often more detrimental to the person that the negative consequences they worried about.

DIVIDE THE FACTS FROM THE ASSUMPTIONS

People may be fearful of the facts, but not anxious. When we don't know what's going to happen we tend to make assumptions, and people typically assume the worst. Very little good will happen if we act upon those assumptions.

DETERMINE WHAT YOU HAVE THE RIGHT OR ABILITY TO CONTROL

You are only responsible for the things you have the right and ability to control. You are not responsible for the things you don't. Your sense of worth is tied only to that which you are responsible for. If you're not living a responsible life, you should feel anxious! Don't try to cast your responsibility onto Jesus — He will throw it back at you. But do cast your anxiety onto Him, because His integrity is at stake in meeting your needs if you are living a responsible and righteous life (see Matthew 6:19–33).

FULFIL YOUR RESPONSIBILITIES

List everything that you can do that is related to the situation that is your responsibility and then commit yourself to do it (Isaiah 32:17).

THE REST IS GOD'S RESPONSIBILITY

The only thing left to do is pray and focus on the truth according to Philippians 4:6–8. Any leftover anxiety is probably due to your assuming responsibilities that God never intended you to have.

ADDITIONAL RESOURCES TO HELP YOU BECOME A FRUITFUL DISCIPLE

Freedom In Christ Ministries has many published resources that can help you in your discipleship journey. You can find details on our websites but here is a selection:

Victory Over the Darkness (Anderson, Bethany House)

The Bondage Breaker (Anderson, Harvest House)

Freedom From Fear (Anderson & Miller, Harvest House)

Overcoming Depression (Anderson, Bethany House)

Winning the Battle Within (Anderson, Harvest House)

Overcoming Addictive Behaviour (Anderson & Quarles, Bethany House)

Setting Your Marriage Free (Anderson, Bethany House)

Restoring Broken Relationships (Anderson, Bethany House)

The Victory Series (Eight Volume Discipleship Curriculum by Anderson, Bethany House)

The Power of Presence (Anderson, Monarch)

The Freedom In Christ app for Android and iOS contains useful teaching, key lists of biblical truth and a structured way to renew your mind.

ADDITIONAL RESOURCES TO HELP OTHERS BECOME FRUITFUL DISCIPLES

Freedom In Christ Ministries exists to equip church leaders to make fruitful disciples who are making a real impact.

There are a number of video-based discipleship courses for churches to use:

The Freedom In Christ Course (Anderson & Goss, Monarch)

The Grace Course (Goss, Miller & Graham, Monarch)

Disciple – the Message of Freedom in Christ for the Millennial Generation (Monarch)

Freedom in Christ for Young People (Monarch)

Freed To Lead (Woods & Goss, Monarch)

You will also find these books useful:

Discipleship Counseling (Anderson, Bethany House)

Becoming A Disciple-Making Church (Anderson, Bethany House)

Setting Your Church Free (Anderson & Mylander, Bethany House)

For further information and to find your nearest Freedom In Christ Ministries office visit:

www.FICMinternational.org.

Printed in the USA
CPSIA information can be obtained
at www.ICGtesting.com
LVHW051154011023
759791LV00016BA/1408